MY TOURIST GUIDE TO THE SOLAR SYSTEM AND BEYOND

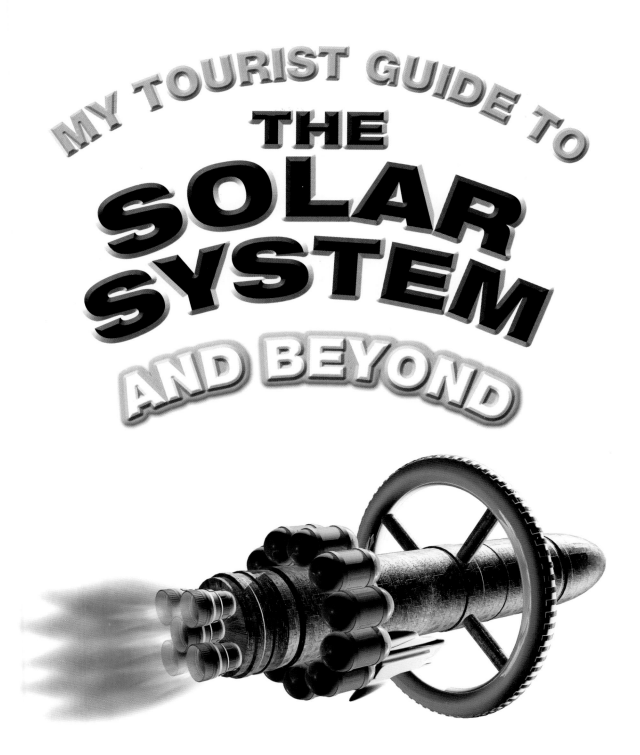

LEWIS DARTNELL

LONDON, NEW YORK, MELBOURNE,
MUNICH, AND DELHI

Senior editor Ben Morgan
Senior art editor Smiljka Surla
Editor Sam Priddy
Designer Riccie Janus
Assistant designer Anna Reinbold
Illustrators Katie Knutton, Maltings Partnership
Production editor Joanna Byrne
Production controller Erika Pepe
Managing editor Julie Ferris
Managing art editor Owen Peyton Jones
Publisher Sarah Larter
Associate publishing director Liz Wheeler
Art director Phil Ormerod
Publishing director Jonathan Metcalf

The author, Dr Lewis Dartnell, is an astrobiologist
and science writer at University College
London's Centre for Planetary Sciences, UK.

First published in Great Britain in 2012 by
Dorling Kindersley Limited
80 Strand, London WC2R 0RL
A Penguin Company

A CIP catalogue record for this book
is available from the British Library
ISBN 978 1 4053 9142 9

Printed and bound in China by Hung Hing
Discover more at
www.dk.com

CONTENTS

4   Get ready to blast off

6   Sun

8   Fly through a sunstorm

10   Mercury

12   Sunrise on Mercury

14   Venus

16   Land on Mount Maxwell

18   Earth

20   Mission to the Moon

22   Mars

24   Hike along the Valles Marineris

26   Trek around Victoria Crater

28   Asteroid belt

30   Jupiter

32   Stormchasing on Jupiter

34   Touchdown on Io

36   Ice diving on Europa

38   Saturn

40   Surf the rings of Saturn

42   Touchdown on Titan

44   The Fountains of Enceladus

46   Uranus

48   Climb the cliffs of Miranda

50   Neptune

52   Have a blast on Triton

54   Pluto

56   Ride a comet

58   Swing by a starbirth nebula

60   Visit a dying star

62   Journey to a black hole

64   Index and acknowledgments

GET READY TO
BLAST OFF

You're about to leave for the holiday of a lifetime: a trip into outer space to see the wonders of the Solar System. You'll be spending most of your time on an interplanetary cruise ship. Space journeys can last months, but don't worry – your ship is packed with features to stop you getting bored and to help you keep fit and healthy in zero gravity.

Recreation sphere
In zero gravity you will be weightless. Dance and play crazy games while floating in the recreation rooms.

Toilets
In space, toilets work like vacuum cleaners, and the waste water is recycled so you can drink it again.

Swimming pool
This room contains a large blob of water for space tourists to swim in.

Bedrooms
Rooms are small and consist of little more than a bed strapped to the wall.

Bridge
The ship's main controls are located at the front of the ship.

Observation dome
Sit back and enjoy amazing views of the Solar System.

Crew quarters
Living areas are located towards the front of the ship – away from the nuclear reactor.

Restaurant
Tables and chairs in the restaurant are bolted to the floor to stop you flying away when you're eating.

Communications dish
This dish sends signals back to Earth so you can keep in touch with friends and family.

SUN

MERCURY

VENUS

EARTH

MARS

ASTEROID BELT

JUPITER

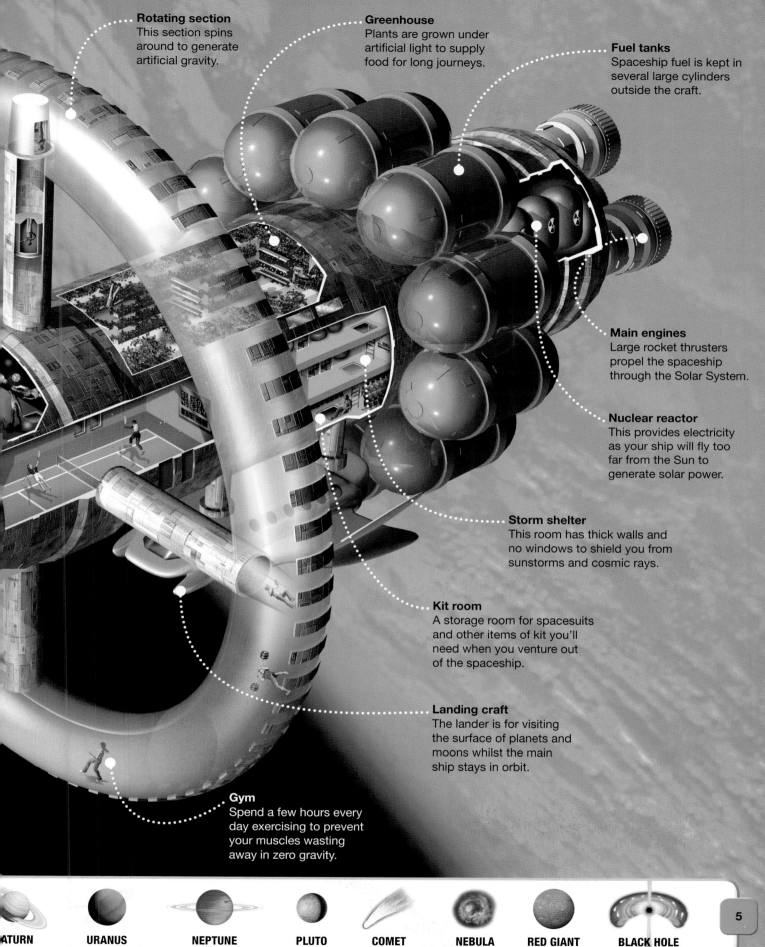

Rotating section
This section spins around to generate artificial gravity.

Greenhouse
Plants are grown under artificial light to supply food for long journeys.

Fuel tanks
Spaceship fuel is kept in several large cylinders outside the craft.

Main engines
Large rocket thrusters propel the spaceship through the Solar System.

Nuclear reactor
This provides electricity as your ship will fly too far from the Sun to generate solar power.

Storm shelter
This room has thick walls and no windows to shield you from sunstorms and cosmic rays.

Kit room
A storage room for spacesuits and other items of kit you'll need when you venture out of the spaceship.

Landing craft
The lander is for visiting the surface of planets and moons whilst the main ship stays in orbit.

Gym
Spend a few hours every day exercising to prevent your muscles wasting away in zero gravity.

ATURN   URANUS   NEPTUNE   PLUTO   COMET   NEBULA   RED GIANT   BLACK HOLE

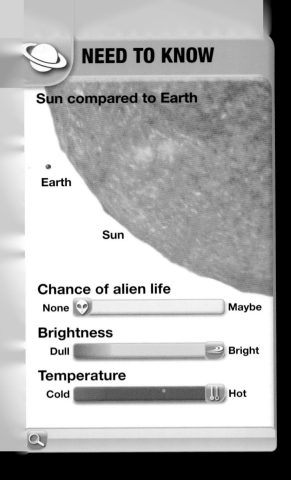

NEED TO KNOW

Sun compared to Earth

Earth

Sun

Chance of alien life

None — Maybe

Brightness

Dull — Bright

Temperature

Cold — Hot

Dark spots
Sunspots are cooler, darker regions that can be many times larger than planet Earth. They are not that cool though – temperatures can still reach 4,000°C (7,200°F).

Atmosphere
The Sun's atmosphere, or corona, stretches for millions of kilometres into space.

SUN

OUR NEAREST STAR

▶ Journey time from Earth: **1 Earth year**

The Sun is our local star. All the planets of the Solar System orbit around it. This gigantic ball of superheated gas (plasma) is a searing 5,500°C (9,900°F) at its dazzlingly bright surface. So for all but the most intrepid adventurers, the Sun is best appreciated from a distance.

THIS STAR PASS ENTITLES THE HOLDER TO A SIZZLING SIX-WEEK STAY EXPLORING THE SUN. SOLAR IMMIGRATION.

SUN
08 MAY 2061

YOU ARE HERE

 SUN

 MERCURY

 VENUS

 EARTH

 MARS

 ASTEROID BELT

 JUPITER

Fiery display
The huge eruptions of plasma in a sunstorm can cause electrical interference back on Earth.

Your spaceship will need a **protective shield** as the Sun gives off harmful **ultraviolet** and **X-ray** radiation.

Every day is a sunny day at the Solar System's star attraction

TOURIST TIP

Solar cruise

"Hot stuff!
Our ship needed a special sunshade to protect our eyes from the intense light. I didn't care though – it still looked amazing."

Activity type: Tour

SAILING THE SOLAR WIND

Hitch a ride across the Solar System on a spaceship driven by the solar wind – the stream of particles flowing out of the Sun and across space at 145 km (90 miles) a second. Attach enormous, flimsy mirror-films to your craft for a relaxing sail through the wonders of space.

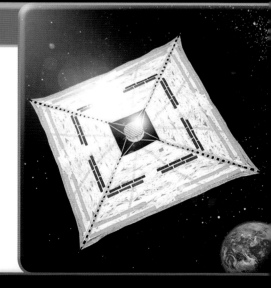

 SATURN
 URANUS
 NEPTUNE
 PLUTO
 COMET
 NEBULA
 RED GIANT
 BLACK HOLE
7

FLY THROUGH A SUNSTORM

The surface of the Sun churns with rising heat and occasionally explodes outwards with unimaginable power in a sunstorm. For the ultimate adventure sport try sundiving. In a specially equipped ship, swoop low above the searing surface and duck through fiery columns and arches held up by magnetic fields. If you're lucky, your pilot might even fly you through a twisting loop of solar plasma.

Giant loops
Solar prominences can be more than 100 times bigger than planet Earth.

Cool plasma
The plasma in a prominence is cooler than the Sun's surface below it.

8

YOU ARE HERE

 SUN

 MERCURY

 VENUS

 EARTH

 MARS

 ASTEROID BELT

 JUPITER

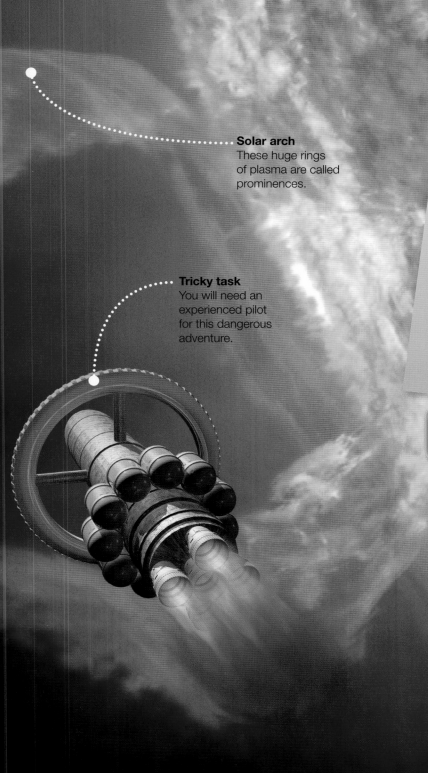

Solar arch
These huge rings of plasma are called prominences.

Tricky task
You will need an experienced pilot for this dangerous adventure.

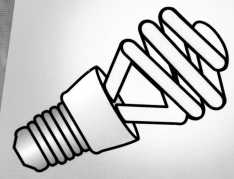

SOLAR POWER

The Sun generates enough energy every second to power human civilization for 500,000 years.

🚀 MAGNETIC STORM

As you swoop close to the Sun you'll notice some of your spaceship's instruments acting strangely. The Sun has an incredibly strong and changeable magnetic field. It twists and turns, creating the impressive sunspots and solar flares that can be seen across the surface.

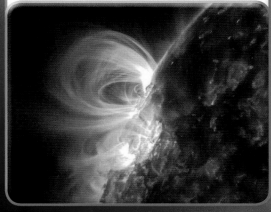

 SATURN   **URANUS**   **NEPTUNE**   **PLUTO**   **COMET**   **NEBULA**   **RED GIANT**   **BLACK HOLE**

NEED TO KNOW

Mercury compared to Earth

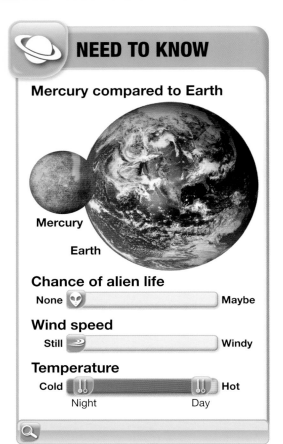

Mercury

Earth

Chance of alien life

None  Maybe

Wind speed

Still Windy

Temperature

Cold Hot

Night   Day

THE SMALLEST PLANET

▶ Journey time from Earth: **5 months**

Mercury is the closest planet to the Sun. It whizzes round the star in only 88 Earth days, giving it the shortest year of any planet. If you enjoy sunbathing Mercury is an ideal destination, with 2,000 hours of sunshine between sunrise and sunset. It takes 176 Earth days between sunrises, so one day on Mercury is twice as long as its year!

Recent impacts ....
Lighter areas on Mercury indicate fresh craters where the surface has been smashed to dust.

EXPLORE CALORIS BASIN

At 1,500 km (900 miles) in diameter Caloris Basin is one of the largest craters in the Solar System. When it formed, almost 4 billion years ago, it sent shockwaves across Mercury, creating strange rock formations on the opposite side of the planet.

Small is beautiful.

Visit the smallest planet in the Solar System for the biggest sunsets!

MERCURIAN MINISTRY OF TOURISM

MERCURY

04 OCTOBER 2049

PLEASE TREAT OUR PLANET WITH RESPECT

Giant crater
The Caloris Basin is nearly one-third the width of Mercury itself.

10

 SUN

YOU ARE HERE MERCURY

 VENUS

 EARTH

 MARS

ASTEROID BELT

 JUPITER

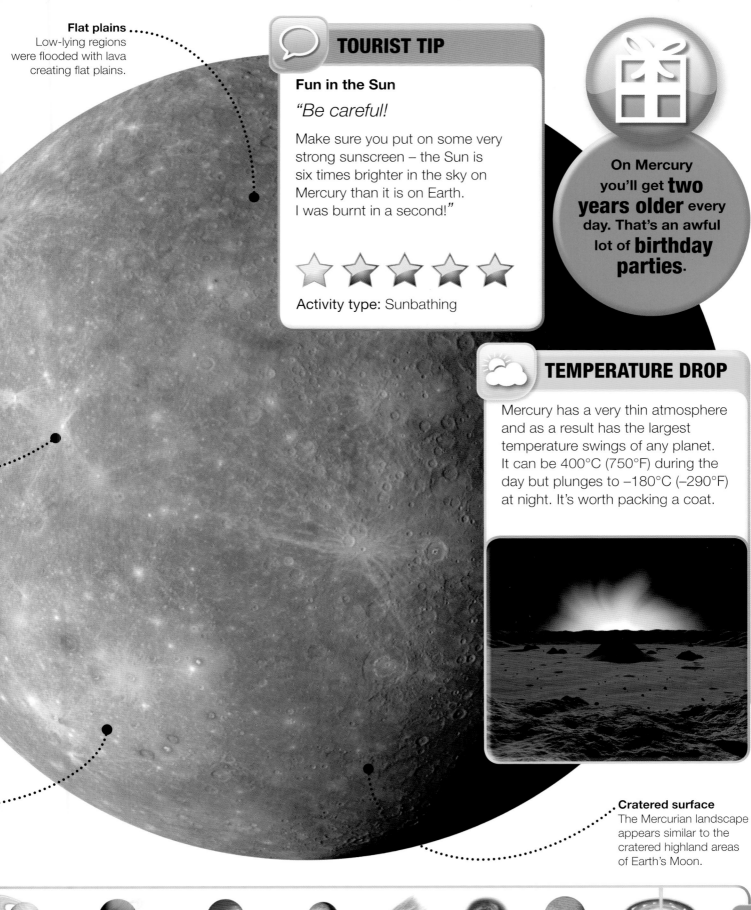

Flat plains
Low-lying regions were flooded with lava creating flat plains.

💬 TOURIST TIP

Fun in the Sun

"Be careful!

Make sure you put on some very strong sunscreen – the Sun is six times brighter in the sky on Mercury than it is on Earth. I was burnt in a second!"

⭐⭐⭐⭐⭐

Activity type: Sunbathing

On Mercury you'll get **two years older** every day. That's an awful lot of **birthday parties**.

☁️ TEMPERATURE DROP

Mercury has a very thin atmosphere and as a result has the largest temperature swings of any planet. It can be 400°C (750°F) during the day but plunges to –180°C (–290°F) at night. It's worth packing a coat.

Cratered surface
The Mercurian landscape appears similar to the cratered highland areas of Earth's Moon.

SATURN   **URANUS**   **NEPTUNE**   **PLUTO**   **COMET**   **NEBULA**   **RED GIANT**   **BLACK HOLE**

SUNRISE ON MERCURY

If you're in the right place at the right time, you can see something amazing on Mercury: a double sunrise. Because Mercury's day is longer than its year, the Sun moves in strange ways across the sky. Seen from the right location, it rises in the morning, dips back below the horizon, and then pops back up again.

TOURIST TIPS

Comet spotting

"*Awesome!*
We watched a comet dive right into the Sun!*"

★★★★☆

Attraction type: Orbital tour

Double sunrise

"*Be patient!*
The double sunrise looked amazing, but the Sun's movement is agonizingly slow – allow at least a month to see it.*"

★★★★☆

Attraction type: Solar display

Crater rim
For a great view across the landscape, climb the rim of any large crater – there are plenty to choose from.

Cool in the shade
The Sun's heat can be ferocious on Mercury, but the temperature in the shade is always well below zero.

SUN

YOU ARE HERE

MERCURY

VENUS

EARTH

MARS

ASTEROID BELT

JUPITER

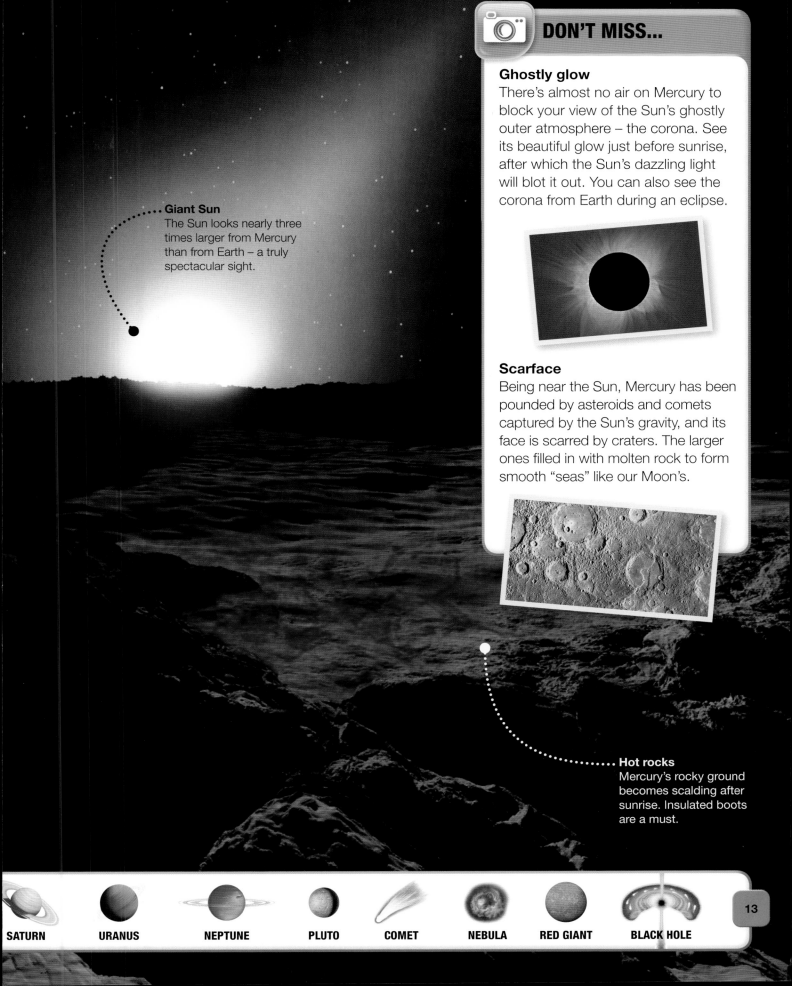

Giant Sun
The Sun looks nearly three times larger from Mercury than from Earth – a truly spectacular sight.

Ghostly glow
There's almost no air on Mercury to block your view of the Sun's ghostly outer atmosphere – the corona. See its beautiful glow just before sunrise, after which the Sun's dazzling light will blot it out. You can also see the corona from Earth during an eclipse.

Scarface
Being near the Sun, Mercury has been pounded by asteroids and comets captured by the Sun's gravity, and its face is scarred by craters. The larger ones filled in with molten rock to form smooth "seas" like our Moon's.

Hot rocks
Mercury's rocky ground becomes scalding after sunrise. Insulated boots are a must.

Venus compared to Earth

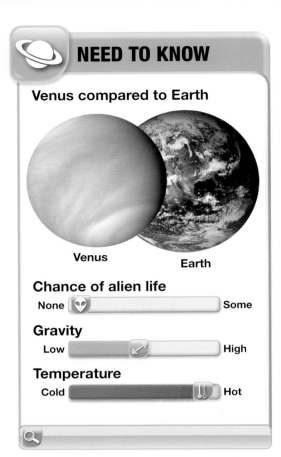

Venus   Earth

Chance of alien life

None ▭ Some

Gravity

Low ▭ High

Temperature

Cold ▭ Hot

VENUS

A PLANET WITH ATMOSPHERE

▶ Journey time from Earth: **2–4 months**

The deadliest of the Solar System's inner planets, Venus is like Earth's evil twin. It's about the same size as Earth and made of the same stuff, but it's hotter than a pizza oven on the surface and the air is so thick it can crush you to death in seconds. You'll need the best safety gear money can buy to visit Venus.

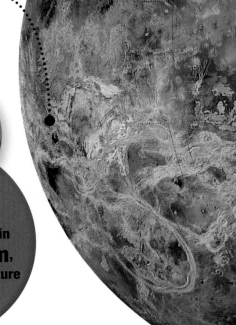

Below the clouds
Dense clouds of acid cover Venus, but this false-colour NASA image reveals what the geography below is like.

Land of volcanoes
The pink areas are highlands, which are packed with towering volcanoes. Eruptions are rare but enormous.

Take a balloon trip

Venus's fast-moving cloud layer will whizz you right round the planet in only four days!

Venus is the **hottest planet** in the **Solar System**, with a surface temperature of **460°C** (860°F).

SUN

MERCURY

YOU ARE HERE

VENUS

EARTH

MARS

ASTEROID BELT

JUPITER

TOURIST TIP

Honeymoon getaway

"Holiday from hell!
We booked our honeymoon here because Venus is named after the Roman goddess of love. But it was more like hell than heaven!"

Activity type: Surface landing

CLOUDY SKY

Venus is smothered by sickly coloured clouds of sulphuric acid. There's never a break in the cloud, so it's permanently overcast below. At the bottom of the cloud layer, the temperature and pressure are about the same as on Earth, which makes this spot a great place to cruise in your ship or take a balloon ride for views of the surface.

Lava plains
Blue areas are flat, rocky plains formed from ancient lava floods.

If you **phone home** from Venus, your voice will take up to **15 minutes** to travel across space to Earth. Stick to **e-mail** if you need to communicate!

Curly canyons
The highlands are riddled with winding valleys where volcanic activity has torn the ground open.

VALID FOR ONE VENUSIAN DAY (243 EARTH DAYS)

VENUS
22 MARCH 2025

THE VISITOR PERMISSION TO LAND ON VENUS

VENUS TOURIST BOARD – THIS STAMP GRANTS

GETTING THERE

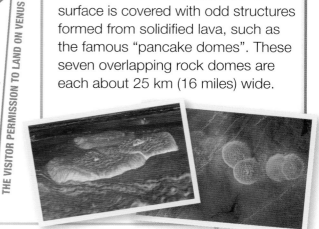

You can get to Venus in a few weeks when the planet is near to Earth in its orbit. Leave at the wrong time, however, and you'll waste a year flying round the Sun.

PANCAKES

Venus is a world of volcanoes. Its surface is covered with odd structures formed from solidified lava, such as the famous "pancake domes". These seven overlapping rock domes are each about 25 km (16 miles) wide.

LAND ON
MOUNT MAXWELL

If you've got the gear to cope with searing heat and crushing pressure, a great spot to land on Venus is Mount Maxwell, the planet's highest point. At 11 km (7 miles) high, its peak is taller than Mount Everest and gives fantastic views. The air is slightly cooler here, with a temperature of only 380°C (716°F) – though that's still hot enough to melt lead.

Under the weather
Don't worry about clouds blocking your view from the mountain – the cloud base on Venus is an amazing 45 km (28 miles) high.

LAVA LAND

Venus's top attractions are its volcanoes. They're everywhere, but nobody is sure how many are active, since the thick clouds block our view from Earth. Bring a camera – you might be lucky enough to snap photos of glowing lava falls or explosive eruptions seen from your vantage point on Mount Maxwell.

Venusian air is so heavy that a gust of wind can **knock you** off your feet. Don't even think about taking a walk if the weather is **windy.**

16

SUN

MERCURY

YOU ARE HERE

VENUS

EARTH

MARS

ASTEROID BELT

JUPITER

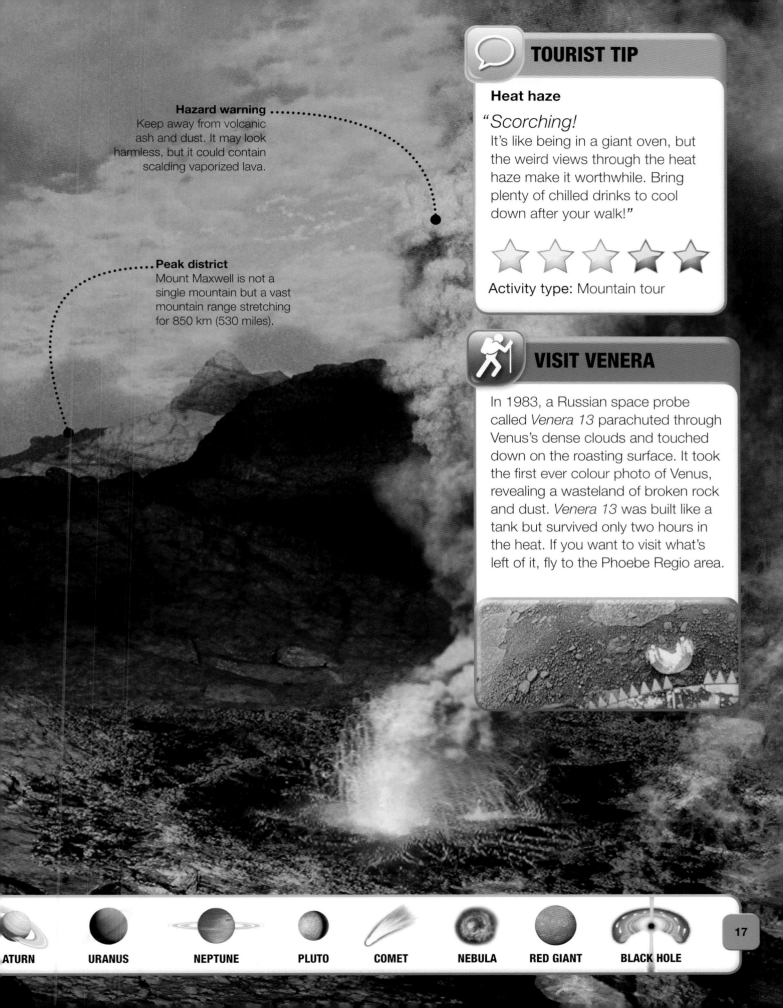

Hazard warning
Keep away from volcanic
ash and dust. It may look
harmless, but it could contain
scalding vaporized lava.

Peak district
Mount Maxwell is not a
single mountain but a vast
mountain range stretching
for 850 km (530 miles).

TOURIST TIP

Heat haze

"Scorching!
It's like being in a giant oven, but
the weird views through the heat
haze make it worthwhile. Bring
plenty of chilled drinks to cool
down after your walk!"

Activity type: Mountain tour

VISIT VENERA

In 1983, a Russian space probe
called *Venera 13* parachuted through
Venus's dense clouds and touched
down on the roasting surface. It took
the first ever colour photo of Venus,
revealing a wasteland of broken rock
and dust. *Venera 13* was built like a
tank but survived only two hours in
the heat. If you want to visit what's
left of it, fly to the Phoebe Regio area.

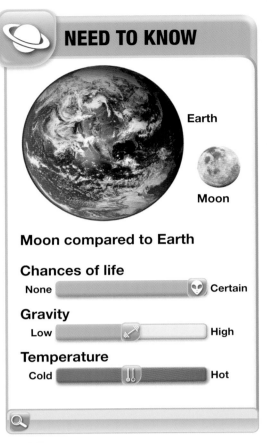

NEED TO KNOW

Earth

Moon

Moon compared to Earth

Chances of life

None ▬▬▬▬▬👽 Certain

Gravity

Low ▬▬▬▬▬ High

Temperature

Cold ▬▬▬🌡▬▬ Hot

EARTH

THE LIVING PLANET

▶ Journey time from Earth: **0 hours**

It may seem boring to some space tourists, but there is no more vibrant planet to visit than our very own Earth. This green and blue world is the only planet in the Solar System that's covered by huge oceans of water and teeming with complex forms of life.

Stormy weather
Cyclones such as this one in the Pacific Ocean tend to form in tropical regions of the planet.

TOURIST TIP

Mid-Atlantic Ridge

"*The floor was moving!*
Earth is the only place in the Solar System where the surface is made up of several moveable plates. We dived down to the bottom of a lake in Iceland to see new crust forming."

★★★★☆

Activity type: Scuba diving

Around **6,000** different **languages** are spoken on Earth – so bring a **phrasebook**.

SUN

MERCURY

VENUS

YOU ARE HERE

EARTH

MARS

ASTEROID BELT

JUPITER

SOLAR ECLIPSE

Even though the Sun is much further away from Earth than the Moon, they appear to be the same size in the sky from Earth due to the Sun's huge diameter. Once in a while the Moon passes in front of the Sun blocking out its light in an incredible solar eclipse.

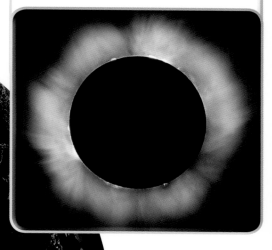

Oceans
Water covers 71 per cent of Earth's surface.

ENJOY LIFE

Earth is the only planet in the Solar System where you're **GUARANTEED** to see living creatures!

EXPLORE METEOR CRATER

Travel to Meteor Crater in Arizona, US, to see one of the most impressive impact craters on Earth. It was created 50,000 years ago by a rock from space. There are fewer craters on Earth than most other planets as its surface is constantly changing due to erosion and geological activity.

MISSION TO
THE MOON

Our Moon is the largest moon in the Solar System relative to its parent planet. There's a lot to see here, from gigantic meteorite craters to "seas" of flat rock formed from lava floods billions of years ago. Only four days away, the Moon is the perfect destination for a short break or for your first experience of an alien world.

Bay of Rainbows
This ancient crater filled up with lava billions of years ago, forming what now looks like a bay.

DON'T MISS

Earthrise
The must-see sight after you arrive in lunar orbit is the view back to Earth. Watch our beautiful blue homeworld emerge like magic over the barren horizon. Not a sunrise, but an Earthrise!

Far side
The Moon always keeps the same face towards Earth, so we don't see its far side – but you can from orbit. The far side has few "seas" but masses of huge craters. Some experts think it was splatted long ago by a second smaller moon that smashed into it.

Hills and hollows
Be sure to take a hike or buggy ride through the Moon's rolling hills, which are found around the rims of the big craters.

Rather than flying in a **straight line** to the Moon, you have to follow a figure-of-eight pattern, first **orbiting** Earth and then orbiting the Moon.

SUN

MERCURY

VENUS

YOU ARE HERE

EARTH

MARS

ASTEROID BELT

JUPITER

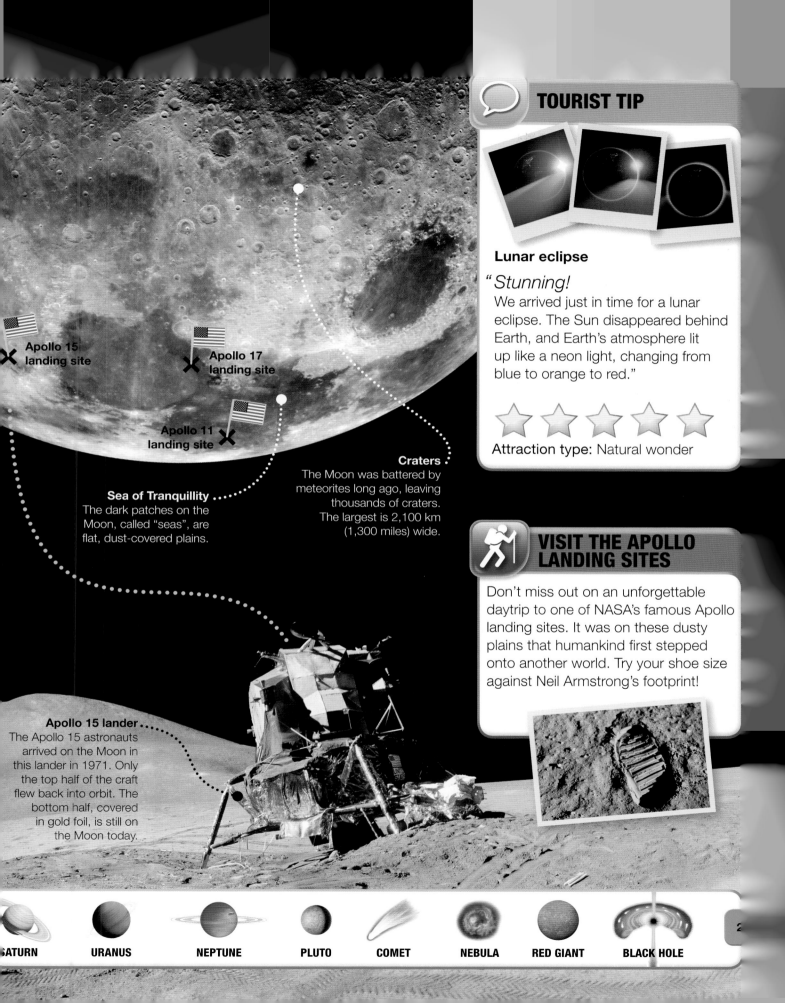

Apollo 15
landing site

Apollo 17
landing site

Apollo 11
landing site

Sea of Tranquillity
The dark patches on the
Moon, called "seas", are
flat, dust-covered plains.

Craters
The Moon was battered by
meteorites long ago, leaving
thousands of craters.
The largest is 2,100 km
(1,300 miles) wide.

Apollo 15 lander
The Apollo 15 astronauts
arrived on the Moon in
this lander in 1971. Only
the top half of the craft
flew back into orbit. The
bottom half, covered
in gold foil, is still on
the Moon today.

TOURIST TIP

Lunar eclipse

"*Stunning!*
We arrived just in time for a lunar
eclipse. The Sun disappeared behind
Earth, and Earth's atmosphere lit
up like a neon light, changing from
blue to orange to red."

Attraction type: Natural wonder

VISIT THE APOLLO LANDING SITES

Don't miss out on an unforgettable
daytrip to one of NASA's famous Apollo
landing sites. It was on these dusty
plains that humankind first stepped
onto another world. Try your shoe size
against Neil Armstrong's footprint!

SATURN   URANUS   NEPTUNE   PLUTO   COMET   NEBULA   RED GIANT   BLACK HOLE

NEED TO KNOW

Mars compared to Earth

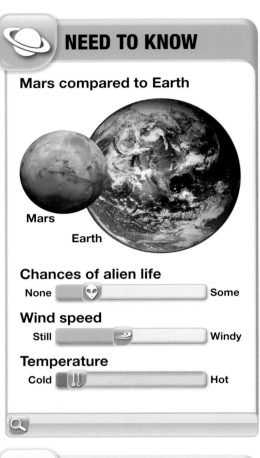

Mars

Earth

Chances of alien life

None [slider] Some

Wind speed

Still [slider] Windy

Temperature

Cold [slider] Hot

DUST STORMS

When Mars is closest to the Sun, huge dust storms appear, sometimes covering the entire planet. Bring goggles so you can see clearly – and find your spaceship.

MARTIAN IMMIGRATION AND CUSTOMS. THIS STAMP ENTITLES TRAVELLER TO STAY ON MARS FOR 30 DAYS.

MARS

06 JUNE 2065

Volcano ....
With huge central craters easily visible from space, the Martian volcanoes are among the most spectacular sights to see from orbit.

Sea of sand ....
A great place to try sand skiing, this vast, sandy plain is dotted with large dunes.

MARS

THE RED PLANET

▶ Journey time from Earth: **7 months**

Mysterious Mars once had water and perhaps even life, but today this small desert world is frozen and dead. Seen from orbit, its face is scarred by huge volcanoes and a vast canyon complex. The dusty sky is pink rather than blue, and the air is too thin to carry sound far, creating an eerie silence.

SUN

MERCURY

VENUS

EARTH

YOU ARE HERE
MARS

ASTEROID BELT

JUPITER

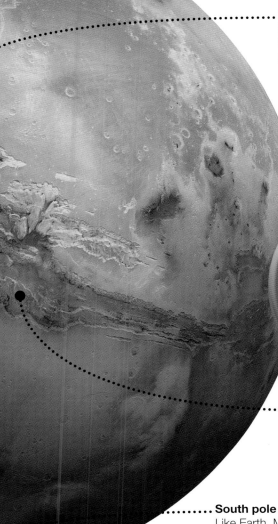

Lost river
In the distant past, water flowed north along this Martian river valley.

Once every two years there's a short **launch window** when Mars is **easiest to reach**. Make sure you're packed in time – you don't want to miss it!

💬 **TOURIST TIP**

Canyon trip

"Fantastic!
Valles Marineris canyon is a must see. We used a buggy to explore the shallower slopes and then flew jetpacks into the deeper gullies! It is 4,000 km (2,500 miles) long though, so it took a while..."

⭐⭐⭐⭐☆

Activity type: Canyon tour

Grand canyons
Called Valles Marineris, this huge canyon complex is Mars's answer to the Grand Canyon on Earth, but it's ten times longer and four times deeper.

South pole
Like Earth, Mars has frosty poles where ice collects in winter. Unlike Earth's polar ice caps, those on Mars are made of carbon dioxide as well as water.

Jump for joy on Mars!

You can jump three times higher on Mars than on Earth due to its weak surface gravity.

🥾 **MOUNTAIN CLIMBING**

The extinct volcano Olympus Mons is three times taller than Mount Everest, making it the largest mountain in the Solar System. It's so big, if you stand at the base you won't be able to see the summit because it will be over the horizon! Hike to the top or land there for stunning views into the crater.

SATURN · URANUS · NEPTUNE · PLUTO · COMET · NEBULA · RED GIANT · BLACK HOLE

HIKE ALONG THE
VALLES MARINERIS

One of the best hiking trips in the Solar System is along the edge of the Valles Marineris canyon. Stretching nearly a quarter of the way around Mars, it makes Earth's Grand Canyon look like a tiny scratch in comparison. The channels appear to have had water flowing down them in ancient times, so look out for fossils.

Landslides
Collapsing loose ground and dust storms continue to shape this canyon.

24

 SUN

 MERCURY

 VENUS

 EARTH

YOU ARE HERE
 MARS

 ASTEROID BELT

 JUPITER

MORNING MIST

If you get up early in the morning you might see mist collecting at the bottom of the valley. It's thought that water that froze on the ground the previous night is vaporized by the morning sun, creating a truly spectacular sight.

This **giant canyon** was named after the *Mariner 9* **space probe** that first photographed it.

Giant cliffs
Layers of sedimentary rock make up the walls of the valley.

Valley depth
Valles Marineris reaches up to 8 km (5 miles) deep in places.

CLIFF JUMP!

Parachute down from one of the highest cliffs. The air is very thin, so bring a supersized parachute to make sure you land in one piece.

 SATURN   **URANUS**   **NEPTUNE**   **PLUTO**   **COMET**   **NEBULA**   **RED GIANT**   **BLACK HOLE**

TREK AROUND
VICTORIA
CRATER

There are thousands of craters on Mars, some of them billions of years old. These scars made by falling space rocks last far longer here than on Earth because there's no rain to wear them away. A great one to visit is Victoria Crater, which is about the size of a football stadium.

Cape Victory

Mini crater
Look out for this mini crater on the rim – it's only a few metres wide.

Sofi Crater

💬 TOURIST TIP

Alien safari

"Boring!
We spent three days looking for alien life, but all we found were rocks. The tour guide said they might contain fossilized bacteria. Whatever!*"

⭐⭐⭐⭐⭐

Attraction type: Safari

0   50 metres
0   100 feet

SUN

MERCURY

VENUS

EARTH

YOU ARE HERE

MARS

ASTEROID BELT

JUPITER

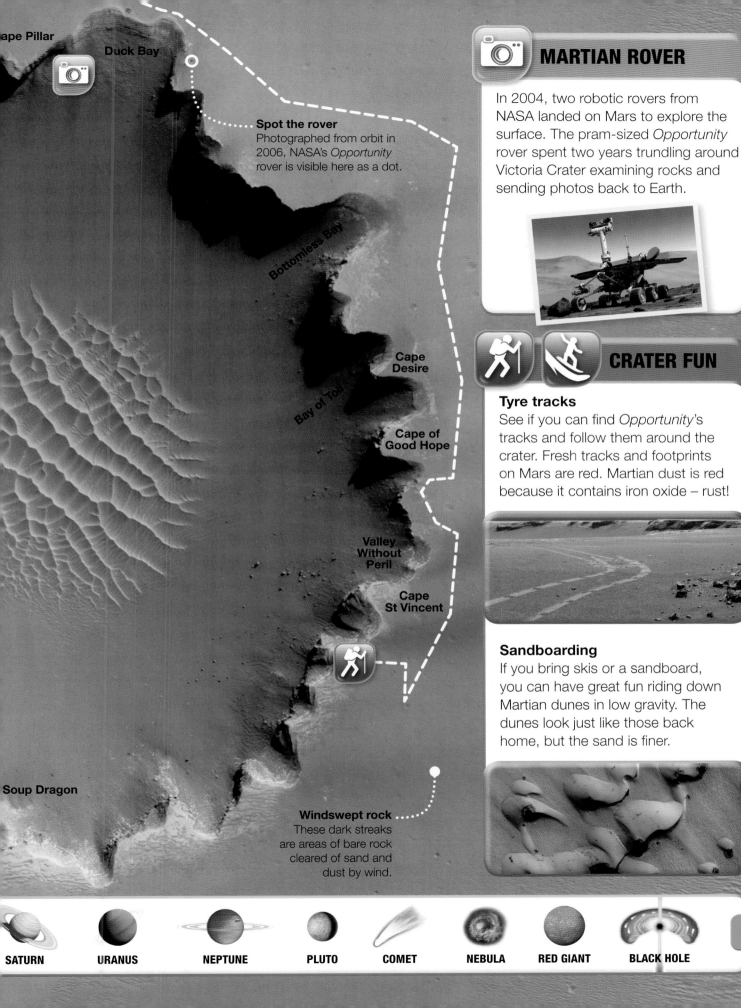

ape Pillar

Duck Bay

Spot the rover
Photographed from orbit in 2006, NASA's *Opportunity* rover is visible here as a dot.

Bottomless Bay

Bay of Toil

Cape Desire

Cape of Good Hope

Valley Without Peril

Cape St Vincent

Soup Dragon

Windswept rock
These dark streaks are areas of bare rock cleared of sand and dust by wind.

MARTIAN ROVER

In 2004, two robotic rovers from NASA landed on Mars to explore the surface. The pram-sized *Opportunity* rover spent two years trundling around Victoria Crater examining rocks and sending photos back to Earth.

CRATER FUN

Tyre tracks
See if you can find *Opportunity*'s tracks and follow them around the crater. Fresh tracks and footprints on Mars are red. Martian dust is red because it contains iron oxide – rust!

Sandboarding
If you bring skis or a sandboard, you can have great fun riding down Martian dunes in low gravity. The dunes look just like those back home, but the sand is finer.

SATURN   URANUS   NEPTUNE   PLUTO   COMET   NEBULA   RED GIANT   BLACK HOLE

Asteroids compared to Earth's Moon

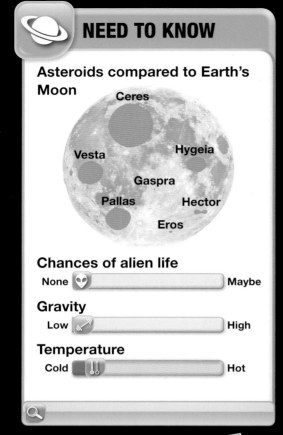

Ceres

Vesta

Hygeia

Gaspra

Pallas

Hector

Eros

Chances of alien life

None — Maybe

Gravity

Low — High

Temperature

Cold — Hot

A MILLION LITTLE WORLDS

▶ Journey time from Earth: **10 months**

As you travel between Mars and Jupiter you'll come across a region of space known as the asteroid belt. Here millions of rocks orbit the Sun. Asteroids are usually too small for gravity to mould them into perfect balls like the planets. Instead they are lumpy and shaped like potatoes.

Gaspra
This was the first asteroid to be studied in detail by a visiting spacecraft.

Some asteroids **rotate** in just a few hours. Standing on one of these **tiny worlds** could make you feel quite **sick**, as the universe appears to **spin** over your head.

Toutatis
Asteroid Toutatis makes a close flyby of Earth every four years.

You'll need a tour guide!

The asteroid belt is mostly empty space. Without a guide you won't see anything!

TOUR GUIDE

ASTEROID BELT TOURISM BOARD, THIS STAMP

GRANTS FREE PASSAGE TO EVERY ASTEROID

ASTEROIDS
1 SEPTEMBER 2083

EXCEPT CERES WHERE AN ADDITIONAL FEE IS REQUIRED

28

 SUN

 MERCURY

 VENUS

 EARTH

 MARS

YOU ARE HERE
 ASTEROID BELT

 JUPITER

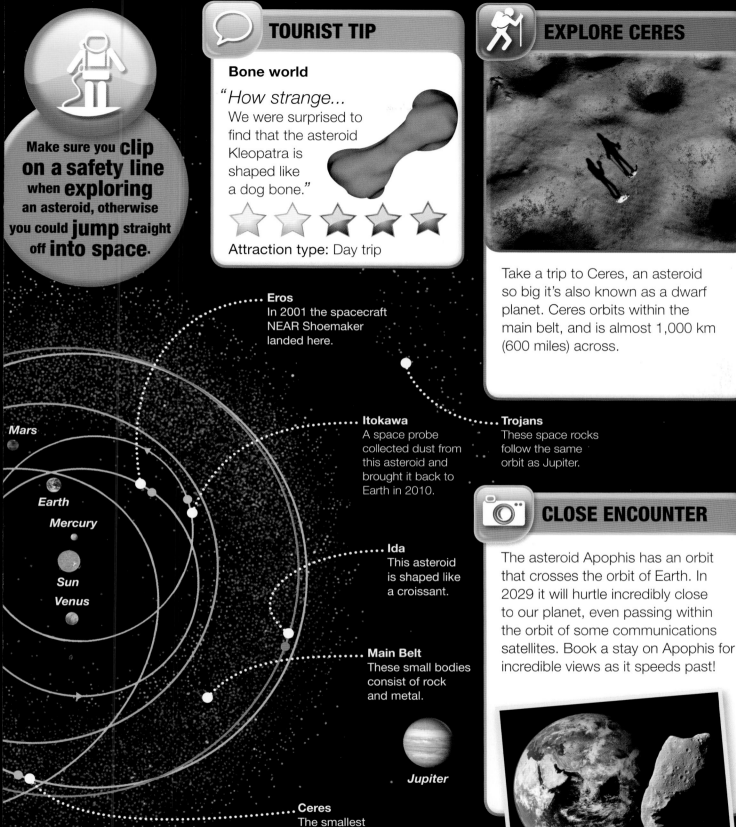

Make sure you **clip on a safety line** when **exploring** an asteroid, otherwise you could **jump** straight off **into space.**

💬 TOURIST TIP

Bone world

"How strange... We were surprised to find that the asteroid Kleopatra is shaped like a dog bone."

⭐ ⭐ ⭐ ⭐ ⭐

Attraction type: Day trip

🥾 EXPLORE CERES

Take a trip to Ceres, an asteroid so big it's also known as a dwarf planet. Ceres orbits within the main belt, and is almost 1,000 km (600 miles) across.

Eros
In 2001 the spacecraft NEAR Shoemaker landed here.

Mars

Itokawa
A space probe collected dust from this asteroid and brought it back to Earth in 2010.

Trojans
These space rocks follow the same orbit as Jupiter.

Earth

Mercury

Ida
This asteroid is shaped like a croissant.

Sun

Venus

Main Belt
These small bodies consist of rock and metal.

Jupiter

Ceres
The smallest dwarf planet in the Solar System.

📷 CLOSE ENCOUNTER

The asteroid Apophis has an orbit that crosses the orbit of Earth. In 2029 it will hurtle incredibly close to our planet, even passing within the orbit of some communications satellites. Book a stay on Apophis for incredible views as it speeds past!

 SATURN    **URANUS**   **NEPTUNE**   **PLUTO**   **COMET**   **NEBULA**   **RED GIANT**   **BLACK HOLE**

29

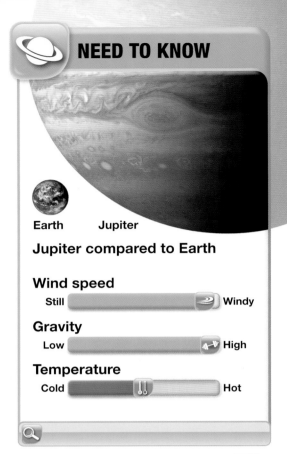

Earth   Jupiter

Jupiter compared to Earth

Wind speed
Still ▭ Windy

Gravity
Low ▭ High

Temperature
Cold ▭ Hot

JUPITER

THE GIANT PLANET

▶ Journey time from Earth: **13 months**

Jupiter is the largest planet in the Solar System and an essential stop-off on your trip. A gas giant, it's a world almost entirely made up of air. Violent storms whip around the planet at incredible speeds, meaning a trip to Jupiter is fraught with danger. While you're here make sure you visit Jupiter's incredible moons Io and Europa.

You'll never get bored on Jupiter

With 63 moons there's plenty to see!

TRIPLE ECLIPSE

The shadows cast by the moons of Jupiter as they pass over its clouds look fantastic. If you're really patient you might catch three moons passing in front of the Sun at the same time in a triple eclipse. This happens once every four years.

Cloud colours
The different colours in Jupiter's clouds come from chemicals such as ammonia, hydrogen sulphide, and water.

Great Red Spot
This hurricane is three times larger than Earth and has been raging for more than 300 years.

Cloud bands
Bands of clouds race around the planet and storms are common where they meet.

North pole
Visit Jupiter's north pole to witness its beautiful auroras.

TOURIST TIP

Asteroid flight

"Scary...
If dodging asteroids is your thing head over to the Trojan asteroids, which share the same orbit as Jupiter. Quite impressive, but I would give it a miss if you've already seen the asteroid belt."

★ ★ ★ ★ ☆

Attraction type: Tour

JOVIAN IMMIGRATION. ENJOY YOUR STAY
ON THE LARGEST PLANET IN THE SOLAR SYSTEM
JUPITER
14 MAY 2029
ANY ISSUES CONTACT OUR HELPDESK OFFICE ON EUROPA

Don't even think about flying close to Jupiter without a very **powerful engine** – you could get **dragged in** by the gigantic planet's **gravity**.

AMAZING AURORA

Put on your ultraviolet goggles to see one of the most incredible sights in the Solar System. Auroras occur on Jupiter's poles when charged particles from the volcanoes of Io collide with the planet's atmosphere.

SATURN   URANUS   NEPTUNE   PLUTO   COMET   NEBULA   RED GIANT   BLACK HOLE

TOURIST TIPS

Colourful clouds

"Mesmerizing!
I could gaze for hours at the churning clouds of Jupiter – they're always changing."

Activity type: Orbital tour

Thunder thrills

"Scary!
After the silence of outer space, the deafening thunder and roaring winds of Jupiter's storms was quite a thrill, but a bit frightening!!"

Activity type: Storm cruise

Jupiter is surrounded by **lethal** radiation. Make sure your radiation **shields** are working or you'll be **DEAD** before you even reach the cloud tops.

Swirly colours
Watch out for the fantastic multicoloured patterns that form between neighbouring bands of cloud.

CLOUD CANYON

For the ultimate thrill, pilot your ship into the "cloud canyon" that surrounds the Great Red Spot. This deep chasm is free of cloud and gives a ringside view of the greatest storm in the known Universe. Just remember to dodge the lightning bolts.

STORMCHASING ON JUPITER

Jupiter looks calm from a distance, but don't be fooled. Fly your ship into the clouds and you'll discover a world of incredible activity. Screaming winds tear through the sky at 400 kph (250 mph), whipping swirling gases and clouds into towering thunderstorms. Brace yourself for lightning bolts more powerful than any on Earth, torrential rain, and blizzards of chemical snow.

Great Red Spot
Don't count on this monster storm actually being red – it keeps changing colour and sometimes fades to white.

In a spin
Watch the Great Red Spot for a while and you'll notice it spins around anticlockwise, dragged by winds moving opposite ways above and below it.

Great white spot
Watch out also for white spots – high storms that float on top of the other clouds. Sometimes two white spots will crash, merge, and change colour.

Io's largest volcanoes spray ash and sulphur **500 km** (310 miles) into space, creating **vast plumes** of falling debris. Bring an iron-clad umbrella!

TOUCHDOWN ON IO

Io is the most tortured moon in the Solar System, its insides being constantly pushed and pulled by the immense force of gravity from nearby Jupiter. This makes Io violently volcanic. It has more than 400 active volcanoes, lakes of bubbling lava, and a surface covered by colourful splotches of sulphur and other chemicals belched out from within it.

34

SUN

MERCURY

VENUS

EARTH

MARS

ASTEROID BELT

YOU ARE HERE

JUPITER

Red hot
The temperature can reach 1,300°C (2,400°F) in Io's eruptions, so keep your distance!

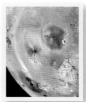

Cosmic pizza
"Smothered in splats of red, orange, and yellow, Io looked a bit like a pepperoni pizza!"

⭐⭐⭐⭐☆

Spot the difference
"Io's surface changes with every eruption. Don't buy a map – it will be out of date by the time you get here."

⭐⭐⭐⭐⭐

Moon walk
It's safe to walk on much of Io. The surface is so cold that falling lava freezes quickly, forming solid ground.

LAVA LAKES
Take a tour of Io's sizzling lava lakes, including gigantic Lake Loki, which is 200 km (120 miles) wide.

"The Jupiter system's hottest attraction!"
Space News

Submarine tour

Take a submarine trip through Europa's hidden ocean and look out for any volcanic hot springs on the sea floor. Some scientists think these may be home to alien life.

Iceberg riding

From time to time, Europa's ocean melts through to the surface, creating a pool of open water that soon freezes over. If you're lucky enough to spot one of these water eruptions, hop a ride on one of the great drifting slabs of iceberg before they all freeze in place again.

Water world

"Utterly incredible!
We didn't find alien life, but the dark ocean under the huge roof of ice was an astonishing sight."

Attraction type: Scuba safari

Scuba gear
You'll need a fully airtight, pressurized diving suit for Europa. The water is exceedingly cold, so your suit will need built-in heating too.

 SUN

 MERCURY

 VENUS

EARTH

MARS

 ASTEROID BELT

YOU ARE HERE

JUPITER

ICE DIVING ON EUROPA

Jupiter's moon Europa is encased in solid ice and has the smoothest surface of all the Solar System's worlds. But beneath this frozen shell is a hidden ocean with more liquid water than all of Earth's seas and lakes combined. Bring diving gear – this is the best place in the Solar System to search for alien life.

Don't worry about **falling** through **thin ice** if you land on Europa's surface. In most places the icy crust is kilometres thick!

Roof of ice
Don't miss the view of the roof of ice over your head. You'll need a torch to see it though – there's no sunlight in Europa's deep dark sea.

GIANT CRACKS

Take a close look at Europa's surface from orbit. You'll see very few craters, but lots of strange, crisscrossing lines that run right around the globe. These are deep cracks in the ground. They are caused by Jupiter's powerful gravity kneading Europa's insides.

SATURN

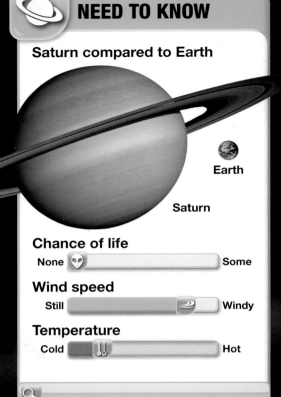

Saturn compared to Earth

Earth

Saturn

Chance of life

None ───────────── Some

Wind speed

Still ───────────── Windy

Temperature

Cold ───────────── Hot

Earth

LORD OF THE RINGS

▶ Journey time from Earth: **2 Earth years**

The second-largest planet in the Solar System, Saturn is a gas giant like Jupiter. It's most famous for its beautiful rings, but it also has a system of more than 60 varied and interesting moons, many of which are worth a trip. If you visit the Saturn system, don't miss the moons Titan and Enceladus.

TOURIST TIP

Saturn flyby

"*Wow!*
The most majestic planet of all, Saturn is the greatest sight in the Solar System. The rings are dazzling when they catch the sunlight yet look paper thin when you fly in line with them. The main planet is fascinating too, with swirling storms and stripes of cloud like Jupiter's."

★ ★ ★ ★ ☆

Attraction type: Saturn system tour

Saturn's shadow
Fly past Saturn's dark side for a stunning view of the rings lit from behind by the Sun.

SUN

MERCURY

VENUS

EARTH

MARS

ASTEROID BELT

JUPITER

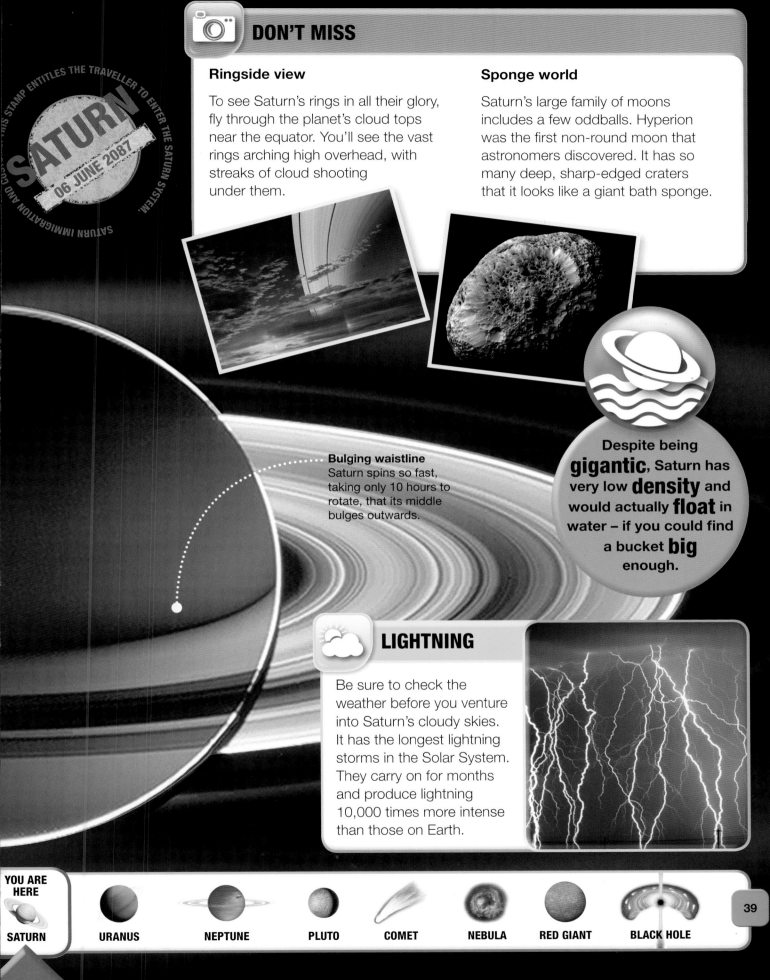

SATURN
06 JUNE 2087

SATURN IMMIGRATION AND CUSTOMS. THIS STAMP ENTITLES THE TRAVELLER TO ENTER THE SATURN SYSTEM.

Ringside view

To see Saturn's rings in all their glory, fly through the planet's cloud tops near the equator. You'll see the vast rings arching high overhead, with streaks of cloud shooting under them.

Sponge world

Saturn's large family of moons includes a few oddballs. Hyperion was the first non-round moon that astronomers discovered. It has so many deep, sharp-edged craters that it looks like a giant bath sponge.

Bulging waistline
Saturn spins so fast, taking only 10 hours to rotate, that its middle bulges outwards.

Despite being **gigantic**, Saturn has very low **density** and would actually **float** in water – if you could find a bucket **big** enough.

LIGHTNING

Be sure to check the weather before you venture into Saturn's cloudy skies. It has the longest lightning storms in the Solar System. They carry on for months and produce lightning 10,000 times more intense than those on Earth.

Cassini Division

"Watch out!
This looks like a huge black gap in the rings, but it actually contains lots of small boulders. I wish someone had warned me!*"*

⭐ ⭐ ⭐ ⭐ ⭐

Attraction type: Orbital tour

JET SET!

Fly a jet pack through the gaps in Saturn's rings to see the rings from both sides.

"A unique way to view this incredible wonder"

Ringmaster
Saturn is 7,000 km (4350 miles) below its closest rings.

Pockmarks
The ice particles are covered in pockmarks from collisions with each other.

SURF THE RINGS OF
SATURN

One of the best reasons to visit Saturn is to see its phenomenal rings. Made up of millions of chunks of ice, they sparkle in the light of the Sun, creating one of the most beautiful sights in the Solar System. Don't miss a spectacular ride through this natural wonder.

Ice boulder
You can land on the largest blocks of ice, which are as big as a house.

YOU ARE HERE
SATURN
URANUS
NEPTUNE
PLUTO
COMET
NEBULA
RED GIANT
BLACK HOLE

TOUCHDOWN ON TITAN

Saturn's moon Titan is giant-sized, even larger than the planet Mercury. It is the only moon to have a thick atmosphere and the sky is filled with dense orange smog. The perfect destination for sailing holidays, Titan is the only place in the Universe other than Earth that we know has lakes and oceans on its surface. They aren't filled with water though, but with liquid chemicals such as methane and ethane.

Take to the skies

The thick air and low gravity on Titan means you can strap wings to your arms and fly away!

Titan's surface
Titan is so cold that water is frozen as hard as stone and makes up much of the moon's landscape.

 SUN

 MERCURY

 VENUS

 EARTH

 MARS

 ASTEROID BELT

 JUPITER

WEIRD RAIN

The rainstorms are huge here so pack a good umbrella. It's strange though – because of Titan's low gravity and thick atmosphere the rain droplets grow to the size of marbles and then drift gently down to the ground.

Orange smog
Titan is a dark and gloomy world because smog blocks out most of the sunlight.

 Methane lakes
These lakes are perfect for a relaxing boat trip.

The liquid in the lakes is **much lighter** than water. If you fell **overboard** you'd **sink** pretty quickly, especially wearing a **heavy spacesuit.**

YOU ARE HERE

  SATURN

 URANUS

NEPTUNE

 PLUTO

 COMET

 NEBULA

 RED GIANT

 BLACK HOLE

43

Saturn's rings
One of Saturn's rings is formed of ice from the fountains of Enceladus.

GLITTER BALL

Don't miss the stunning views of Enceladus glittering in the sunlight when you're in orbit around this moon. Look out also for the dark "tiger stripes" where the icy crust has split.

Ice canyon
The fountains erupt from deep valleys called tiger stripes, which give Enceladus a stripey appearance when seen from space.

TOURIST TIP

Fountain tour

"Awe-inspiring!
A mind-blowing sight. The ice gushes out of the ground at an amazing speed, and with no air and little gravity to slow it down, it seems to keep on rising forever."

Attraction type: Natural wonder

Gravity is so weak on Enceladus, you'll weigh less than a pineapple does on Earth. Make sure you **harness** yourself to the ground so you don't go flying off!

SUN

MERCURY

VENUS

EARTH

MARS

ASTEROID BELT

JUPITER

THE FOUNTAINS OF ENCELADUS

If you want to visit some of Saturn's 62 moons, Enceladus should be top of your list. This tiny, ice-coated moon is the shiniest, whitest world in the Solar System. Astronomers used to think it was just a boring snowball, but in 2005 they discovered huge eruptions of glittering ice from valleys in its surface – the fountains of Enceladus.

Eruption site
The fountains are fed by an underground salty sea near the moon's south pole.

AROUND THE MOON IN ONE DAY

Take a snowmobile trip and drive right round tiny Enceladus in just 24 hours. Mind the cracks though!

YOU ARE HERE

 SATURN

 URANUS

 NEPTUNE

 PLUTO

COMET

 NEBULA

 RED GIANT

 BLACK HOLE

45

URANUS

THE SIDEWAYS PLANET

▶ Journey time from Earth: **4 Earth years**

Uranus is possibly the most boring planet in the Solar System. You can't visit its surface and there aren't any storms – just a plain covering of blue-green clouds of methane. There is something unusual about Uranus, though: it's the only planet in the Solar System to roll along on its side rather than spinning around upright. If you're stuck for things to do, head to Uranus's moon Miranda where you can climb the tallest cliffs in the Solar System.

Cloud cover
The white bands in Uranus's atmosphere are the highest clouds.

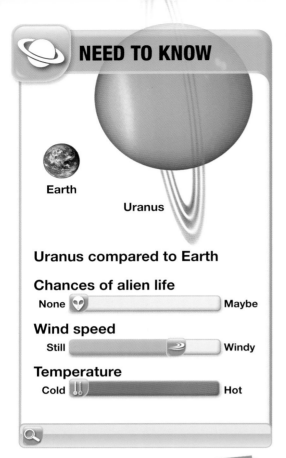

NEED TO KNOW

Earth

Uranus

Uranus compared to Earth

Chances of alien life

None   Maybe

Wind speed

Still   Windy

Temperature

Cold   Hot

Chill out on Uranus

It's the coldest planet in the Solar System. Temperatures get as low as –224°C (–371°F).

WACKY SEASONS

Because Uranus rolls around on its side, it has some extremely unusual seasons. Each pole gets 42 years of continuous daylight followed by 42 years of night. Bear this in mind when planning your trip – it's much more interesting on the sunny side.

SUN   MERCURY   VENUS   EARTH   MARS   ASTEROID BELT   JUPITER

Brightest ring
Epsilon is the outermost of Uranus's inner rings, and also the brightest.

URANUS
19 JANUARY 2066

WELCOME TO URANUS – A RELAXING HOLIDAY DESTINATION. NO TERRIFYING STORMS OR SCARY VOLCANOES HERE.

Uranus is
3 billion km
(1.8 billion miles) from
the **Sun** and takes
84 years to **orbit** it.

BULLSEYE

It's not only Uranus that has been tipped over, but its rings and all of its moons too. Look out of your ship window as you approach the planet and you'll see the faint rings tilted towards you like a giant bullseye.

Blue planet
Methane crystals in the atmosphere absorb red light making Uranus blue.

CLIMB THE CLIFFS OF MIRANDA

The best of Uranus's icy moons is Miranda, which has the tallest cliffs anywhere in the Solar System. Pack your ice axe and crampons and have a go at scaling the 8 km (5 mile) tall cliff face – the views over the moon and beyond are breathtaking. To get back down, simply jump off the top and fall all the way. In the weak gravity it will take seven minutes to get to the bottom, but you'll need a jetpack to break your fall.

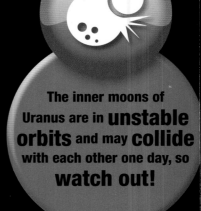

The inner moons of Uranus are in **unstable orbits** and may **collide** with each other one day, so **watch out!**

Twilight world
The Sun is so far from Miranda that daylight feels more like twilight. Bring a torch to find the way.

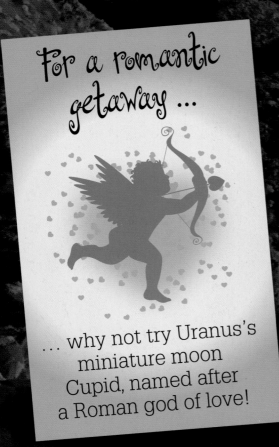

For a romantic getaway ...

... why not try Uranus's miniature moon Cupid, named after a Roman god of love!

SUN

MERCURY

VENUS

EARTH

MARS

ASTEROID BELT

JUPITER

Uranus's rings
The view of Uranus and its faint rings is spectacular from Miranda's surface.

💬 TOURIST TIPS

Uranus has 27 known moons. Here are reviews of some of the largest.

Ariel
"The brightest of Uranus's mostly dark moons, Ariel has deep canyons filled with glittering ice."

⭐⭐⭐⭐⭐

Titania
"Titania is named after a fairy queen in a Shakespeare play. It's the ideal place to send arty postcards from!"

⭐⭐⭐⭐⭐

Oberon
"Weird – if you look at the Sun from Oberon, the Sun goes round and round in the sky in small circles."

⭐⭐⭐⭐⭐

SATURN

YOU ARE HERE

URANUS

NEPTUNE

PLUTO

COMET

NEBULA

RED GIANT

BLACK HOLE

49

NEPTUNE

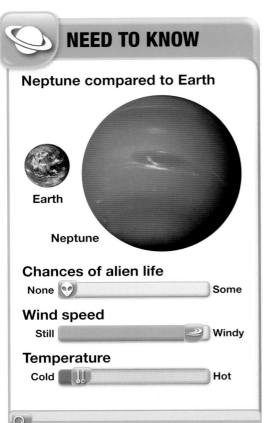
THE WINDY WORLD

▶ Journey time from Earth: **8 Earth years**

Neptune is the furthest planet from the Sun and it is not for the faint-hearted. Freezing, perilous storms rage throughout Neptune, unlike its relatively calm neighbour Uranus, making it a dangerous place to visit. While here, make sure you stop off at the nearby moon Triton to visit its fantastic geysers.

Blue planet ·········
Neptune appears blue because the methane in the upper atmosphere absorbs the red light from the Sun, but reflects the blue light.

Neptune is a **gas planet**, so it doesn't have a solid surface. **Don't try and walk on it** – you'll plunge thousands of kilometres to the rocky core.

stay forever young on Neptune

One year on Neptune lasts **165 Earth years**, so you'll always stay your current age!

50

SUN

MERCURY

VENUS

EARTH

MARS

ASTEROID BELT

JUPITER

TOURIST TIP

Neptune's rings

"Disappointing!
I was looking forward to seeing Neptune's rings, but they're so dark it was hard to make them out. Saturn's rings are way better."

★☆☆☆☆

Attraction type: Tour

DIAMOND RAIN

Far beneath your spaceship in Neptune's gas interior, there are showers of gemstones falling like rain. The extreme heat and pressure can transform the methane gas into diamonds.

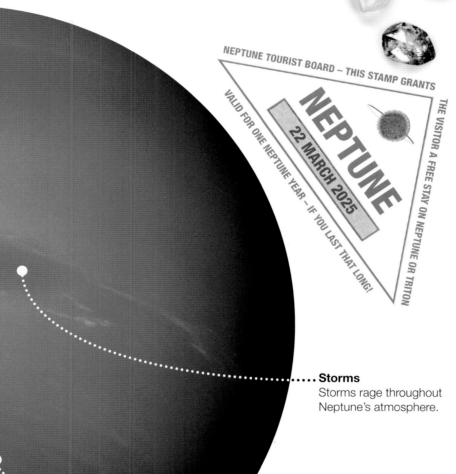

Storms
Storms rage throughout Neptune's atmosphere.

Cloud bands
A bit like Jupiter, Neptune has bright and dark cloud bands running round the planet.

SOAR THROUGH THE ATMOSPHERE

Take to the skies with a hang glider and catch the powerful winds in Neptune's atmosphere. They are the strongest in the Solar System, reaching 2,000 kph (1,250 mph), so brace yourself for a hair-raising ride.

HAVE A BLAST ON
TRITON

Do you want to get your feet back onto solid ground? Visit Triton, Neptune's largest moon. Its volcanic geysers are one of the natural wonders of the Solar System. Stand back and watch as nitrogen gas erupts up to 8 km (5 miles) above Triton's scarred face. Don't worry if you arrive on Triton later than expected – each eruption can last for up to a whole Earth year so you'll have plenty of time to soak up the view.

Erupting gas
The nitrogen gas that erupts from the geysers is quickly blown away by the wind.

Geyser debris
The geysers leave dark streaks on Triton's surface that stretch for hundreds of kilometres.

52

 SUN

 MERCURY

 VENUS

 EARTH

 MARS

 ASTEROID BELT

 JUPITER

TOURIST TIPS

Neptune has 12 other moons you can also visit. Here are the best of the bunch.

Proteus
"We visited a really cool crater that was more than 200 km (124 miles) in diameter."

Neso
"Terrible journey. We had to travel 48 million km (30 million miles) from Neptune just to get here. It took ages…"

Naiad
"We couldn't stay long because it's going to smash into Neptune's atmosphere soon!"

Orbiting Neptune
Triton is the only large moon in the Solar System that orbits in a different direction to its planet's rotation.

 SATURN

 URANUS

YOU ARE HERE
 NEPTUNE

 PLUTO

 COMET

 NEBULA

RED GIANT

 BLACK HOLE

53

Pluto compared to Earth

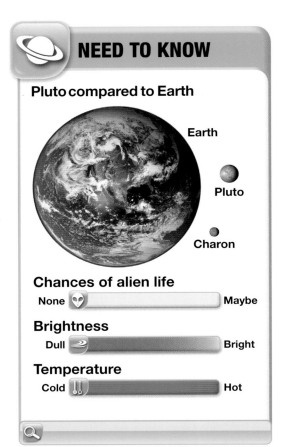

Earth

Pluto

Charon

Chances of alien life
None — Maybe

Brightness
Dull — Bright

Temperature
Cold — Hot

PLUTO

....

THE DWARF PLANET

▶ Journey time from Earth: **9-10 Earth years**

Pluto is a small and frosty world lurking in the outer Solar System. You'll notice that Pluto's moon Charon is extremely large in comparison to Pluto – they're like double worlds twirling around each other. In 2006, astronomers decided that Pluto wasn't a proper planet but a dwarf planet, along with Eris and Ceres, but it's still well worth a visit.

STARLIGHT

When you finally reach Pluto the Sun will look like no more than a bright star in the sky, and as a result it's dark on Pluto's surface. It's easy to get lost on Pluto – bring a torch to help you explore.

EXPLORE THE KUIPER BELT

The region that's home to Pluto is bigger and better than the Asteroid Belt!

Patchy surface ......
Different parts of Pluto are covered in water ice, frozen nitrogen, and frozen methane.

SUN

MERCURY

VENUS

EARTH

MARS

ASTEROID BELT

JUPITER

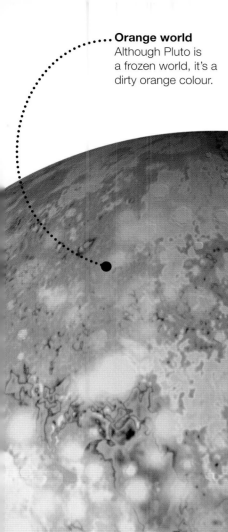

Orange world
Although Pluto is a frozen world, it's a dirty orange colour.

If you're planning to go ice skating make sure you **cool** your skates down first. The frozen nitrogen could **explode** beneath your feet with just a little **warmth**.

SLEDGE RIDE

Head over to Charon to go sledging. Unlike Pluto, its surface consists mostly of water ice, which makes for a safer ride. The gravity is far lower on Charon than on Pluto though, so be careful not to sled off into space.

TOURIST TIP

Short stay on Pluto

"Cold and dark… I don't know why I bothered – Pluto isn't even a planet anymore! I'd recommend visiting the dwarf planet Eris instead – it's bigger."

Attraction type: Tour

ENITTILES YOU TO A FOUR-MONTH STAY ON PLUTO   THE BEST DWARF PLANET IN THE SOLAR SYSTEM

PLUTO
22 OCTOBER 2103

YOU MIGHT AS WELL VISIT CHARON WHILST YOU'RE HERE

TWIN TAILS

Most comets have two tails pointing in slightly different directions. The brightest tail is made of dust and curves back along the comet's orbital path. The second tail, which is often blue, is made of gas and always points directly away from the Sun, whichever way the comet is flying.

Choose your comet **carefully** – some comets don't just **swoop** around the **Sun** – they **crash** into it!

RIDE A COMET

Comets are big lumps of dirty ice that normally lurk unseen in the outer Solar System but occasionally come swooping close to the Sun. As a comet nears the Sun, it warms up and comes to life. Ice and dust erupt from its surface to form a huge, glowing cloud around the comet and spectacular tails. If you've got plenty of time on your hands, you can hitch a ride on a comet in the outer Solar System and travel all the way round the Sun.

SUN

MERCURY

VENUS

EARTH

MARS

ASTEROID BELT

JUPITER

LAND ON A COMET

Make sure you land on the solid core, or nucleus, of the comet. It's best to do this while the comet is in the outer Solar System, beyond Jupiter. Once it gets as close to the Sun as Mars, its fragile surface will begin to break up, releasing fountains of gas and dust that will cloud your view. The icy surface of the comet is actually pretty dark because the ice contains lots of other chemicals, including amino acids – the building blocks of life.

Tall tails
The tails of comets can grow millions of kilometres long as comets near the Sun but disappear when comets fly back to the outer Solar System.

Mind your feet when **strolling** on a comet – **sudden eruptions** of gas can happen without warning and **blast** you into space!

TOURIST TIP

Comet landing

"Dirty snowball
A comet is like a giant snowball, so we thought it would be the ultimate place for a snowball fight. But there was so much muck around that the snow was black."

Activity type: Comet cruise

SATURN

URANUS

NEPTUNE

PLUTO

YOU ARE HERE

COMET

NEBULA

RED GIANT

BLACK HOLE

57

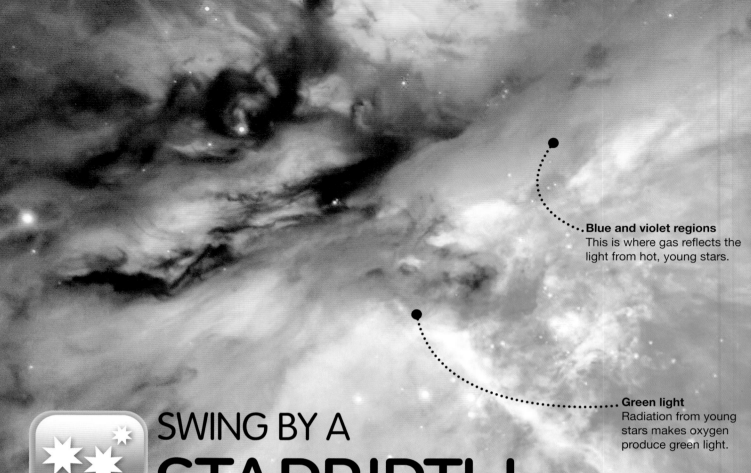

Blue and violet regions
This is where gas reflects the light from hot, young stars.

Green light
Radiation from young stars makes oxygen produce green light.

SWING BY A
STARBIRTH
NEBULA

▶ Journey time from Earth: **20 million Earth years**

Seen from Earth a nebula is just a blurry smudge, but as you approach one you'll see it is actually a vast colourful cloud of gas and dust. The Orion Nebula is situated in the Orion constellation. Thousands of new stars and the planets that orbit them are forming in regions of the cloud.

SUN

MERCURY

VENUS

EARTH

MARS

ASTEROID BELT

JUPITER

NEW PLANETS

Many young stars have dusty discs swirling around them, where new planets are forming. Visit one to witness the birth of a new world. Some of these planets may one day evolve life of their own.

Red regions
Radiation from new stars makes hydrogen glow red.

TOURIST TIP

Pillars of Creation

"*Absolutely incredible!*

We visited the Eagle Nebula in the Serpens constellation to see the Pillars of Creation. Stars were forming within the gigantic columns of gas, and we could see some poking out of the top."

⭐ ⭐ ⭐ ⭐ ☆

Activity type: Sightseeing

The **Orion Nebula** is **1,300 light years** away from **Earth**. A light year is how far **light can travel** in one year.

SATURN

URANUS

NEPTUNE

PLUTO

COMET

YOU ARE HERE

NEBULA

RED GIANT

BLACK HOLE

59

TRAVEL TIP

Red giant tour

"Spooky!
The starlight makes everything look blood red – it's really spooky! It was a very long trip, but we spent most of it asleep in deep freeze."

Attraction type: Interstellar cruise

 ## SUPERNOVA

When Betelgeuse reaches the very end of its life, it will self-destruct in an explosion brighter than a billion suns – a supernova. Its core will then collapse under gravity until it's only a few kilometres wide. Betelgeuse could explode any time in the next million years. When it does, it will outshine the Moon in Earth's night sky.

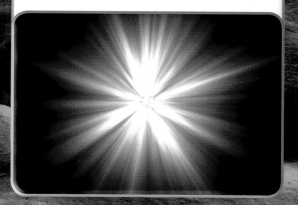

Betelguese is one of the **largest red giants** known. If you swapped it with the **Sun**, its surface would reach all the way to Jupiter!

Scorched planet
The heat of a red giant or supergiant turns nearby planets into scalding, waterless desert worlds. One day, this will happen to Earth.

 SUN

 MERCURY

 VENUS

 EARTH

 MARS

ASTEROID BELT

 JUPITER

VISIT A DYING STAR

Once a star runs out of fuel, it begins to die. Its outer layers puff outwards enormously and cool to a red colour. The star becomes a "red giant" or a "red supergiant" – a bloated, dying star hundreds of times bigger than our Sun. Betelgeuse (pronounced "beetle juice") is one of the nearest red supergiants and well worth a visit.

Supersize star
As a dying giant star swells up, it swallows the planets and moons around it.

🚀 GETTING THERE

Betelgeuse is in the constellation of Orion, and you can see its reddish colour easily from Earth. The star is 640 light years from Earth, which means that its light takes 640 years to cross space to reach your eyes. Your ship can't travel anywhere near as fast as light speed. At the speed of NASA's fastest-ever space probe, it would take you 10 million years to fly to Betelgeuse.

Betelgeuse

JOURNEY TO A
BLACK HOLE

When a gigantic star dies, all its matter gets sucked by gravity into a single point that's tinier than a full stop. The star turns into a black hole, a dark monster with such powerful gravity that not even light can escape its clutches. Only the most daring space tourist should consider flying near a black hole.

Point of no return
Anything crossing this line is trapped inside the black hole forever – even light. Astronomers call the line the "event horizon".

🚀 LONG-HAUL FLIGHT

The nearest black hole is 6,000 light years away from Earth. Travelling at the speed of NASA's *Voyager* spacecraft, it will take you 94 million years to get there. Your body will have to be frozen during this long voyage, so you don't age.

Doomed stars
Some black holes tear apart and suck in the stars around them, growing ever more powerful as they swallow more matter.

📷 GALACTIC CENTRE

At the centre of our galaxy is a black hole so massive that it weighs more than a billion Suns. The black hole itself is invisible, but it's surrounded by a violent whirlpool of debris from torn up stars.

SUN

MERCURY

VENUS

EARTH

MARS

ASTEROID BELT

JUPITER

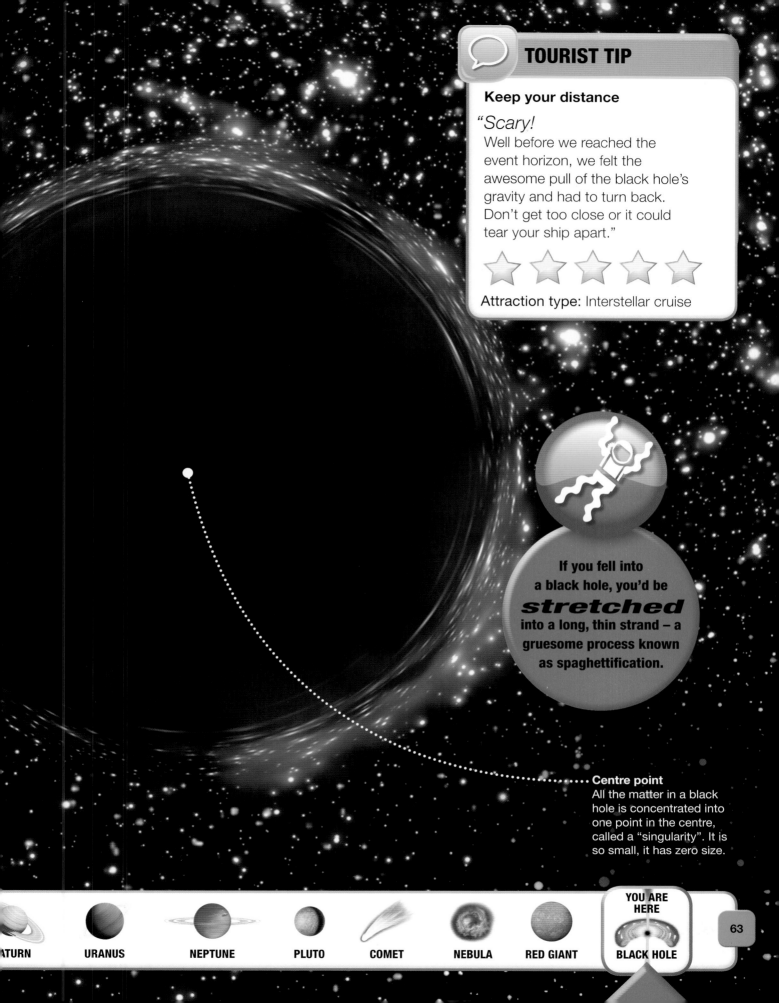

If you fell into a black hole, you'd be **stretched** into a long, thin strand – a gruesome process known as spaghettification.

Centre point
All the matter in a black hole is concentrated into one point in the centre, called a "singularity". It is so small, it has zero size.

INDEX

A

Acid clouds 14, 15
Apollo missions 21
Apophis 29
Ariel 49
asteroid belt 28–29
asteroids 13, 28, 29, 31
atmosphere 6, 11, 42
auroras 31

B

Betelgeuse 60, 61
black holes 62–63

C

Caloris Basin, Mercury 10
canyons 44, 49
Mars 22, 23, 24–25
Venus 15
Cassini Division 40
Ceres 29, 54
Charon 54, 55
cliffs 48–49
cloud bands 31, 32, 38, 51
cloud canyons 32
clouds 30, 46
Venus 14, 15, 17
comets 12, 13, 56–57
corona 6, 13
craters:
    Mars 26–27
    Mercury 10, 11, 13
    Meteor Crater 19
    moons 21, 39, 53
Cupid 48

D

days 10, 12
density 39

diamonds 51
dust storms 22, 24
dwarf planets 29, 54–55

E

Eagle Nebula 59
Earth 18–19
Earthrise 20
eclipses 13, 19, 21, 30
Enceladus 38, 44–45
Eris 54
Eros 29
Europa 30, 34–35
event horizon 62

G H

gas giants 30, 38
gas planets 50
Gaspra 28
geysers 36, 50, 52
gravity:
    Jupiter 31, 34, 37
    Mars 23
    moons 42, 44, 48
    Pluto 55
Great Red Spot 30, 32, 33
Hyperion 39

I

ice:
    comets 56
    moons 37, 49, 53
    Pluto 54, 55
    rings 41
ice caps 23
ice fountains 44–45
Ida 29
Io 30, 31, 34–35
Itokawa 29

J K

Jupiter 30–33
Kleopatra 29
Kuiper Belt 54

L

Lake Loki, Io 35
lakes 42, 43
lava 11, 15, 35
life:
    comets 57
    Earth 18, 19
    Mars 22, 26
    moons 37
lightning 32, 33, 39
lunar eclipse 21

M

magnetic fields 8, 9
Mariner 9 probe 25
Mars 22–27
Mercury 10–13
Meteor Crater, Arizona 19
methane lakes 42, 43
Mid-Atlantic Ridge 18
Miranda 46, 48–49
Moon 19, 20–21
moons:
    Jupiter 30, 34–37
    Neptune 52–53
    Pluto 54
    Saturn 38, 39, 42–45
    Uranus 46, 48–49
Mount Maxwell 16–17
mountains 16, 23

N

Naiad 53
nebula 58–59

Neptune 50–51
Neso 53
nitrogen 52

O

Oberon 49
Olympus Mons, Mars 23
Opportunity rover 27
Orion Nebula 58, 59

P

pancake domes 15
Pillars of Creation 59
plasma 8, 9
Pluto 54–55
poles 23, 31, 53
Proteus 53

R

radiation 7, 32
red giants 60–61
rings:
    Neptune 51
    Saturn 38, 39, 40, 44
    Uranus 47, 49
rovers, robotic 27

S

sand dunes 22, 27
Saturn 38–41
seas 13, 20, 21
seasons 46
smog 42, 43
solar eclipse 19
solar flares 8, 9
solar prominences 8
solar wind 7
spaceship 4–5
spaghettification 63

stars 6, 54, 58–61
storms:
    Earth 18
    Jupiter 30, 31, 32–33
    magnetic 8, 9
    Neptune 50, 51
    Saturn 38, 39
sulphur 34
Sun 6–9, 48, 54
sunspots 6, 8, 9
sunstorms 7, 8–9
supernova 60

T U

thunderstorms 32–33
Titan 38, 42–43
Titania 49
Toutatis 28
Triton 50, 52–53
Trojan asteroids 29, 31
Uranus 46–47

V

Valles Marineris 23, 24–25
Venera 13 probe 17
Venus 14–17
Victoria Crater, Mars 26–27
volcanoes:
    Io 34
    Mars 22, 23
    Venus 14, 15, 16

W Y

water:
    Earth 18
    Europa 37
    Mars 22, 23, 24, 25
wind 16, 32, 33, 51
years 10, 12, 50

ACKNOWLEDGMENTS

Dorling Kindersley would like to thank Richard Beatty for proofreading and Chris Bernstein for the index.

The publisher would also like to thank the following for kind permission to reproduce their photographs:
(Key: a-above; b-below/bottom; c-centre; f-far; l-left; r-right; t-top)
Alamy Images: CVI Textures 16clb.
Corbis: Mike Agliolo 10clb; Jonathan Blair 19crb; Yvette Cardozo / Index Stock 36-37; Dennis di Cicco 56clb; Miloslav Druckmuller, Vojtech Rusin / Science Faction 13cra; Larry Dale Gordon 10crb; Mehau Kulyk / Science Photo Library 60clb; Mark Garlick Words & Pictures Ltd / Science Photo Library 40cla; Weatherstock 39crb; Jim Zuckerman 19tr. **Dorling Kindersley:** 50tl,

50-51. **Dreamstime.com:** Diego Barucco 53ftr. **ESA:** NASA / G. Bacon (STScI) 62-63; NASA, and M. Showalter (SETI Institute) 46tl, 47l. **ESO:** L. Calçada / http://creativecommons.org / licenses / by / 3.0 54clb. **Getty Images:** Flickr / Celisa B. M. Serra 21tr; The Image Bank / Werner Van Steen 35cr; Eric Meola 51crb (hang glider); Stocktrek Images 25tc. **NASA and The Hubble Heritage Team (AURA / STScI):** ESA, and E. Karkoschka (University of Arizona) 30c; ESA, John Clarke (University of Michigan) 31br. **Japan Aerospace Exploration Agency (JAXA):** 7crb. **Ron Miller:** 12-13, 15ftr, 16-17, 22bl, 24-25, 29tr, 32clb, 34-35, 39ca, 40-41, 44-45, 48-49, 51tr, 51crb, 52-53, 55cra, 57cr, 60cl, 60-61, 62crb. **NASA:**

9crb, 17crb, 21br, 24cl, 53tr; Cassini Imaging Team / SSI / JPL / ESA 38-39; Cassini-Huygens / JPL / Space Science Institute 39cra; ESA / Paolo Nespoli / Dmitry Kondratyev 4-5 (background); ESA / SOHO 6-7; Goddard Space Flight Center Image by Reto Stöckli (land surface, shallow water, clouds). Enhancements by Robert Simmon (ocean color, compositing, 3D globes, animation). Data and technical support: MODIS Land Group; MODIS Science Data Support Team; MODIS Atmosphere Group; MODIS Ocean Group Additional data: USGS EROS Data Center (topography); USGS Terrestrial Remote Sensing Flagstaff Field Center (Antarctica); Defense Meteorological Satellite Program (city lights) 10tl, 14tl, 18tl, 22tl (Earth), 30tl

(earth), 38tl (Earth), 46fcla, 50ftl, 54tl; GSFC / NOAA / USGS 18-19; Dr Joe Gurman / US SOHO Project Scientist / NASA Goddard Space Flight Center 6tl; Jeff Hester and Paul Scowen Arizona State University 59br; Jet Propulsion Laboratory (NASA-JPL) 27tr; Jet Propulsion Laboratory / California Institute of Technology, Pasadena, CA / David Seal 46crb; Johns Hopkins University Applied Physics Laboratory / Carnegie Institution of Washington 11c, 13cr; Johnson 20cl; JPL 15br, 15fbr, 30clb, 32-33, 37br; JPL / DLR 30cl; JPL / Mosaic by Mattias Malmer 15tr; JPL / NSSDC Photo Gallery 36ca; JPL / Space Science Institute 30tl, 30-31, 38ftl, 44cl; JPL / University of Arizona 27br, 35tc, 35tr, 36clb, 53tl; JPL / USGS 14-15, 20-21tl; JPL-Caltech / Cornell University 27cr; JPL-Caltech / T. Pyle (SSC) 59cra; JPL-Caltech / University of Arizona / Cornell / Ohio State University 26-27;

Lunar and Planetary Institute 20-21b; Mariner 10; Astrogeology Team, U.S. Geological Survey 10ftl; NSSDC / GSFC 20bl; Stephen Ostro et al. (JPL), Arecibo Radio Telescope, NSF 29tc; SDO / AIA 8-9; Viking Project 22tl (Mars), 22-23; Voyager 2 47crb. **naturepl.com:** Wild Wonders of Europe / Lundgre 18bl. **Science Photo Library:** Chris Butler 56-57; Russell Croman 58-59; David Ducros 15cr; Walter Myers 11crb; John Sanford 61crb. **Luc Viatour (www.lucnix.be) (CC BY-SA 3.0):** http://creativecommons.org/licenses/by/3.0 19ca.

End papers: Corbis: Robert Llewellyn

All other images © Dorling Kindersley
For further information see:
www.dkimages.com